# PARENTING THE STORM

## A Guide to Helping Kids Navigate Big Feelings!

KEISHA MCDONALD MA, MS, LPC

1st editionBook Design: Keisha McDonald-Griffin
Production: AmourLegaci Publishing
Editing: Keisha McDonald
Illustrations: Web designs
Publisher: AmourLegaci Publishing
To order: maddtherapy.com, Amazon.com, Barnes & Noble, Amourlegacipublishing.com
Author Website: Amourlegacipublishing.com
Printed in United States of America

# PARENTING
# THE
# STORM

## A Guide to Helping Kids
## Navigate Big Feelings!

KEISHA MCDONALD MA, MS, LPC

STORM WARNING

# TABLE OF CONTENTS

# Introduction

As parents, one of the most important skills we can teach our children is how to regulate their emotions. Just like learning to read or ride a bike, managing emotions is a skill that takes time, patience, and practice. This guide will help you understand your child's emotional development and provide simple, effective strategies to support them through big feelings.

Parenting the Storm Guide isn't for the faint of heart—especially when emotions run high. Whether you're raising a fiery toddler, a sensitive child, or a moody teenager, emotional outbursts can feel like storms rolling through your home. ome are loud and sudden, others quiet and slow-moving, but all leave an impact.

Parenting the Storm was created to help you navigate these emotional weather patterns with greater understanding, patience, and skill. It's not about controlling your child's feelings—it's about guiding them through those feelings with calm, clarity, and consistency.

Inside, you'll find:

- Tools to help children and teens identify and manage their emotions in real time
- Practical strategies for when emotions escalate and logic takes a backseat
- Tips for creating safe, structured environments where emotional growth can thrive
- Support for you, the parent, as you weather the storm alongside your child

No child comes with a manual, but emotional regulation can be taught—and you don't have to do it alone. This guide will walk with you, equipping you to be the steady anchor your child needs when emotions feel too big to handle.

# Chapter 1:

# What Is Emotion Regulation?

# What Is Emotion Regulation?

Emotions are a natural part of being human. However, for children, understanding and managing emotions can be overwhelming. Emotion regulation is the ability to recognize, understand, and control emotions in a healthy way. It's a crucial skill that helps children navigate relationships, handle challenges, and build resilience.

# Why Is Emotion Regulation Important?

- Helps children develop healthy relationships with peers and family.
- Supports academic success by improving focus and problem-solving skills.
- Reduces stress and anxiety by teaching coping mechanisms.
- Encourages self-confidence and independence in decision-making.

## How Do Children Process Emotions at Different Ages?

Children's ability to regulate emotions evolves as they grow. Understanding their developmental stage can help you provide the right support.

- **Toddlers (1-3 years)**: Express emotions through tantrums and need comfort and guidance to learn coping strategies.
- **Preschoolers (3-5 years)**: Begin to label emotions but may struggle with impulse control.
- **Early Elementary (5-7 years)**: Can recognize different emotions but may still need help managing strong feelings.
- **Preteens (8-12 years)**: Develop more independence in emotion regulation but benefit from structured guidance.
- **Teens (13-17 years)**: Teens process emotions differently than children or adults because their brains—and especially the parts responsible for emotional regulation—are still developing.

# Emotional Suppression vs. Healthy Regulation

- **Emotional Suppression**: Ignoring or pushing emotions away, which can lead to stress and frustration.

- **Healthy Emotion Regulation**: Acknowledging emotions and using coping skills to manage them in a constructive way.

# Why Do Some Kids Struggle More?

While all children experience emotional ups and downs, some may have a harder time regulating emotions due to:

- **Temperament**: Some children are naturally more sensitive or reactive.
- **Environment**: Stressful home situations or lack of emotional modeling can make regulation difficult.
- **Neurological Differences**: Children with ADHD, anxiety, or sensory processing challenges may need extra support.

# Emotional Suppression
## vs.
# Healthy Regulation

Adolescence brings a unique set of emotional challenges. Teen emotions will be addressed separately throughout each chapter to provide focused guidance and support.

This guide will equip you with practical tools to help your child and your teen navigate and regulate their emotions—and offer insight on how you, as a parent, can respond with confidence and clarity. By understanding the basics of emotion regulation parents can create a supportive environment that encourages healthy emotional growth. In the next chapter, we'll explore the science behind emotions and how the brain processes feelings.

—

*I let go of what I can't change and do my best with what I can.*

—

# Chapter 2:

# The Science Behind Emotions

Emotions don't just appear out of nowhere— they have a biological foundation that influences how we react, feel, and behave. Understanding how emotions work in the brain and body can help parents support their children in managing big feelings.

# How the Brain Processes Emotions

The brain plays a key role in how we experience and regulate emotions. Three major parts work together to shape our emotional responses:

- Amygdala: The brain's "alarm system" that detects threats and triggers strong emotions like fear and excitement.

- Prefrontal Cortex: The "thinking brain" that helps regulate emotions, control impulses, and make decisions.

- Hippocampus: The memory center that helps us connect past experiences with present emotions.

## Brain Development: Still in Progress

Adolescence is an emotional rollercoaster—for teens and the adults raising them. Between brain development, hormonal changes, and the quest for identity, teenagers are navigating emotional terrain that's intense, confusing, and often overwhelming.

As a parent, your role isn't to "fix" their feelings but to understand them, guide them, and model healthy emotional regulation.

**Brain Development:**
Still in Progress

**Here's what you need to know:**

**The Teen Brain is Still Under Construction**

- **Amygdala vs. Prefrontal Cortex:** Teens rely more on the amygdala *(the emotional center of the brain)* than the prefrontal cortex *(responsible for logic, impulse control, and long-term planning)*. This means emotions often feel intense and immediate, and they may struggle to pause and think through their feelings.

- The prefrontal cortex continues maturing into the mid-20s, so emotional regulation is a work in progress.

- Teens process emotions through the amygdala, the part of the brain that reacts quickly and emotionally—think fight, flight, or freeze.

- The prefrontal cortex, which manages judgment, self-control, and reason, is still developing and won't be fully mature until their mid-20s.

**What this means for parents:** Expect big emotions and impulsive reactions. Stay calm and consistent, even when they aren't.

When children experience strong emotions, their amygdala may take over, making it harder for them to think rationally. That's why young kids often need guidance to calm down before they can talk about their feelings.

# The Role of Hormones and the Nervous System

Hormones also influence emotions. When children feel stressed, their bodies release cortisol, the stress hormone, which prepares them to react quickly. On the other hand, hormones like **dopamine and oxytocin** promote happiness and social bonding.

The nervous system has two main parts that impact emotional responses:

- **Sympathetic Nervous System**: Activates the body's "fight-or-flight" response in stressful situations.
- **Parasympathetic Nervous System**: Helps the body relax and return to a calm state after stress.

Teaching children strategies like deep breathing and mindfulness helps activate their **parasympathetic nervous system**, making it easier for them to calm down when overwhelmed.

# Teen Hormones
## Fuel
# Emotional Intensity

- Puberty brings hormone shifts that make emotions feel stronger and more unpredictable.

- One minute they're fine, the next they're slamming doors or sobbing. They're not trying to be dramatic—it's just where their bodies and brains are.

**What this means for parents:**

Don't take emotional swings personally. Offer space when needed and stay available for connection afterward.

# The Connection Between Emotions, Behavior, and Learning

Emotions and behavior are closely linked. When children feel safe and regulated, they can focus, problem-solve, and engage in learning. But when emotions are out of control, behavior may become reactive, and learning becomes difficult.

**Key connections:**

- Emotional stress can reduce focus and make it hard to absorb information.
- Positive emotions boost learning by increasing motivation and memory retention.
- Emotional regulation skills improve social interactions and classroom behavior.

By understanding the science behind emotions, parents can better support their children in managing feelings effectively. In the next chapter, we'll explore common emotional challenges children face and how to help them navigate big emotions.

# Chapter 3:

# Common Emotional Challenges in Children

Children experience a wide range of emotions daily, but some feelings can be particularly challenging to manage. Understanding these common emotional struggles can help parents provide the right support.

# Anxiety and Worry

- Fear of the unknown, social situations, or failure can trigger anxiety.
- Symptoms may include excessive worry, restlessness, trouble sleeping, or avoiding certain situations.
- Encouraging open conversations and teaching relaxation techniques can help ease anxious feelings.

# Frustration and Anger

- Children often feel frustrated when things don't go their way.

- Younger children may have tantrums, while older kids may express anger through defiance or withdrawal.

- Teaching problem-solving skills and healthy outlets for anger (like physical activity or deep breathing) can prevent emotional outbursts.

# Meltdowns vs. Tantrums: Understanding the Difference

- Tantrums are intentional outbursts used to gain attention or get something desired.

- Meltdowns happen when a child is emotionally overwhelmed and unable to process their feelings.

- Responding with patience and providing a calm-down space can help children recover from meltdowns more quickly.

# Sadness and Disappointment

- Children may struggle with losses, unmet expectations, or changes in routine.

- Signs include withdrawal, crying, or a lack of interest in usual activities.

- Helping kids label their emotions and validate their feelings encourages resilience.

# How Unmet Needs Contribute to Emotional Outbursts

- Sometimes big emotions stem from basic needs like hunger, fatigue, or overstimulation.

- Ensuring children have regular meals, rest, and downtime can reduce emotional struggles.

- Teaching children to recognize their needs and express them can improve self-regulation.

# Peer Relationships Carry Heavy Emotional Weight

*TEEN*

- Belonging matters more than ever. Peer approval or rejection can make or break their emotional state.

- Friendships, social media, romantic interests—these are central to their world and deeply impact how they feel.

**What this means for parents:**
Be a safe, nonjudgmental sounding board. Don't downplay social stress. Help them process without shaming or preaching.

By recognizing and addressing these emotional challenges, parents can help children develop the tools they need to navigate their feelings effectively. In the next chapter, we'll dive into practical strategies to teach kids healthy coping skills for managing emotions.

# Chapter 4:

# Teaching Kids Healthy Coping Skills

Helping children manage their emotions starts with giving them the right tools. Just like learning to read or ride a bike, emotional regulation is a skill that takes practice. In this chapter, we explore simple but effective techniques to help kids handle big feelings in a healthy way.

# 1. Deep Breathing Exercises

Teaching children to control their breathing can help them calm down when they feel overwhelmed. Try these fun breathing techniques:

- **Balloon Breaths** – Imagine inflating a big balloon by taking a deep breath in through the nose, then slowly exhaling through the mouth.
- **Square Breathing** – Inhale for four seconds, hold for four seconds, exhale for four seconds, and pause for four seconds before repeating.
- **Bunny Breaths** – Take three short sniffs through the nose, then exhale one long breath through the mouth, just like a bunny sniffing!

## 2. The Calm-Down Corner

Creating a safe, cozy space where kids can go when they feel upset helps them regain control.

This space can include:

✅ Soft pillows or a weighted blanket
✅ Stress balls or fidget toys
✅ A feelings chart to help them express emotions
✅ Headphones for calming music

# 3. The Power of Movement

Physical activity is a great way to release pent-up emotions.

**Encourage kids to:**

- Dance to their favorite song
- Go for a short walk outside
- Try yoga poses like "child's pose" or "butterfly stretch"
- Do simple stretches or jumping jacks

# 4. Journaling and Drawing Emotions

Some children express themselves better through art or writing.

**Encourage them to:**

📝 Keep a "Feelings Journal" where they write or draw their emotions

🎨 Create an "Emotion Wheel" with different faces to represent feelings

🖍 Draw a comic strip showing how they handled a tough situation

## 5. The Self-Talk Strategy

Negative thoughts can make emotions feel even bigger.

**Teach your child to use positive self-talk to calm themselves:**

🚫 Instead of: "I'm bad at this."
✅ Try: "I'm learning, and I'll get better!"

🚫 Instead of: "This is too hard."
✅ Try: "I can take a deep breath and try again."

🚫 Instead of: "I always mess up."
✅ Try: "Mistakes help me learn."

# Teens are
## Learning Who
### They Are

• Teens are working through questions of identity, self-worth, and independence. Emotional reactions may stem from struggles with confidence, fear of failure, or internal pressure to figure it all out.

**What this means for parents:**

Validate their experiences, even if they don't make sense to you. Encourage self-expression through journaling, creativity, or honest conversations.

By practicing these techniques, kids can build lifelong skills to manage their emotions with confidence and resilience.

# Chapter 5:

# Building Emotional Resilience

Emotional resilience is the ability to recover from setbacks, adapt to change, and keep going in the face of challenges. It doesn't mean kids won't feel sadness, anger, or frustration—it means they can move through those emotions and learn from them.

# 1. Encourage a Growth Mindset

Help your child see mistakes and challenges as opportunities to grow:

- Use phrases like "You can't do it yet" or "Every mistake is a chance to learn."

- Celebrate effort, not just outcomes.

## 2. Practice Problem-Solving Together

Teach your child to break down problems into smaller steps:

- What happened?
- How do you feel?
- What are three things we could do?
- What's the best choice right now?

Role-playing common situations helps build this skill in a safe, supportive way.

# 3. Teach Coping Strategies

Provide your child with healthy tools for managing stress, like:

- Deep breathing or guided imagery
- Journaling or drawing their feelings
- Getting outside for a change of scenery
- Talking to a trusted adult

# 4. Help Reframe Negative Thoughts

Kids often think in extremes —"This is the worst day ever!"

**Help them reframe:**

- "What else could be true?"
- "What would you say to a friend who felt this way?"
- "Can you name something that went well today?"

# They Don't
## Have All the
### Coping Tools—Yet

Most teens haven't been taught how to regulate their emotions in healthy ways.

They might:
- Shut down or isolate
- Lash out verbally or physically
- Seek relief through risky behavior

**What this means for parents:**

- Teach them emotional vocabulary ("I'm overwhelmed," "I feel rejected," etc.).
- Model calm under pressure.
- Introduce coping tools like deep breathing, physical activity, or talking things out.

Resilient kids learn to challenge negative self-talk and bounce back stronger. The following pages offer practical coping strategies to help you support your child or teen in managing their emotions in the moment.

# Chapter 6:

# Creating a Supportive Emotional Environment

Children thrive in environments where they feel safe, seen, and supported. Your home and relationships provide the foundation for emotional growth.

# 1. Model Emotion Regulation

Children learn by watching you. When you express emotions calmly and manage stress in healthy ways, they're more likely to do the same.

- Narrate your feelings: "I'm feeling frustrated, so I'm going to take a few deep breaths."
- Apologize and repair after moments of overreaction —this shows that mistakes are human and fixable.

## 2. Build Predictable Routines

Routines create a sense of stability that helps kids feel secure:

- Keep regular meal, bedtime, and homework times.
- Prepare kids for transitions with warnings: "In 10 minutes, we're leaving the park."

Knowing what to expect helps reduce emotional overwhelm.

# 3. Make Room for All Feelings

Create a family culture that welcomes all emotions—even the hard ones.

- Say: "It's okay to feel angry, but it's not okay to hurt others."
- Avoid: "Don't cry" or "Calm down!" Instead try: "Take your time, I'm here."

Validating feelings builds trust and emotional intelligence.

# 4. Communicate Openly

Ask open-ended questions and listen without judgment:

- "What was the best part of your day?"
- "Is something bothering you that you want to talk about?"

Use everyday moments to stay connected emotionally.

## 5. Use Praise Thoughtfully

Focus on praising effort, kindness, and emotional awareness:

- "I noticed you took a deep breath when you got frustrated—that was awesome."
- "You were really patient with your little brother. That was kind."

## They Still Need You—
## Even When They Push
## You Away

Teens may seem distant, moody, or even hostile, but they still need connection, structure, and guidance.

**What this means for parents:**
Stay consistent with boundaries. Be present, even in silence. Offer love without conditions.

———

## Quick Tips for Supporting Teen Emotion Regulation

- Listen first. Let them vent without jumping to solutions.
- Name emotions. Help them identify what they're feeling.
- Stay calm. Model the emotional control you want them to develop.
- Set boundaries. Emotions don't excuse disrespect or harm.
- Encourage healthy outlets. Journaling, art, movement, prayer, or safe conversation.

Normalize the struggle.
Remind them emotional ups and downs are part of growing up.

# Chapter 7:

# YOUR Role in Modeling Emotion Regulation

Children are always observing. They learn more from what we do than what we say. That's why modeling emotion regulation is one of the most powerful tools we have.

## 1. Show, Don't Just Tell
- Express your own feelings in a calm, age-appropriate way: "I'm feeling overwhelmed, so I'm going to take a break."
- Let your child see you use coping skills in real time—breathing, walking away to cool down, or journaling.

## 2. Be Honest, Not Perfect
- You don't need to hide your emotions. It's okay to say, "I'm having a hard day."
- When you lose your temper or make a mistake, model repair: "I'm sorry I snapped. I was feeling stressed. Let's talk about it."

## 3. Stay Curious About Your Own Triggers
- Notice what sets off your reactions and explore why.
- The more emotionally aware you are, the easier it is to respond with intention, not just react.

## 4. Practice Self-Care
- You can't pour from an empty cup. Prioritize rest, connection, and stress relief.
- Explain your self-care to your child: "I'm going for a walk because it helps me clear my mind."

# Final Word to Parents

Teen emotions can be loud, messy, and confusing—but they're also a sign of growth. Your job isn't to protect your child from hard feelings, but to teach them how to move through those feelings with honesty, strength, and resilience.

Be patient.
Stay anchored.
You're shaping an emotionally healthy adult,
one conversation at a time.

# Chapter 8:

# Using Everyday Moments to Teach Emotional Awareness

Emotional education doesn't just happen during meltdowns or serious talks. It happens in tiny, everyday moments—if we know where to look.

## 1. Narrate Feelings Throughout the Day
- "You look really proud of that drawing!"
- "That must have been frustrating when the tower fell."
- "I can see you're feeling shy. That's okay—let's take our time."

## 2. Use Books, Movies, and Stories
- Pause during stories to ask: "How do you think they're feeling?"
- Reflect on the ending: "What did the character learn about their emotions?"

## 3. Play Emotion Games
- Feelings charades, emotion memory cards, or sorting faces into categories like happy, sad, angry, etc.
- These make emotional learning fun and interactive.

## 4. Celebrate Emotional Wins
- "You got really mad and didn't yell—you took a breath instead. That was amazing."
- Reinforce progress, not perfection.

# Final Words

Emotions can be overwhelming—for children and parents alike. But every meltdown, every tear, every tense moment is also an opportunity: to teach, to connect, and to build emotional resilience that will last a lifetime.

Parenting the Storm isn't about perfection—it's about presence. It's about showing up with calm when chaos rises. It's about being the safe place your child can return to while they learn how to navigate the waves inside them.

# Final Words cont...

**Remember:**

- You don't have to have all the answers.
- You won't always get it right.
- But your consistency, love, and willingness to grow alongside your child make all the difference.

By guiding your child through their emotions instead of around them, you're equipping them with the tools they need to thrive—not just now, but well into adulthood.

Keep going. Keep anchoring. You're not just parenting through the storm—you're teaching them how to rise above it.

They may not remember every word you said, but they will remember how safe they felt with you in their hardest moments.

**Dear Caregiver,**

Thank you for showing up—for reading, coloring, reflecting, and practicing alongside your child. Emotion regulation isn't about being perfect; it's about being present. You are your child's safe space, teacher, and greatest support.

There will be tough days, and there will be wins—big and small. Celebrate each step forward. The time and care you've put into this journey matters. Your love and effort help create a future where your child feels seen, heard, and confident navigating their world.
Keep going. You're doing amazing work.

With care and encouragement,

**MADD Therapy Team** 🌟

Congratulations on completing Parenting the Storm - A Guide to Helping Kids Navigate Big Feelings! You've taken a powerful step in nurturing emotional growth for your child—and for yourself. The tools you've learned and the conversations you've started will continue to strengthen your relationship, build resilience, and foster lifelong emotional well-being.

## Continue the Journey

- Keep practicing emotion naming and regulation strategies
- Use the printables regularly to reinforce skills
- Revisit chapters whenever you or your child face new challenges

# Fun Self-Care Challenges
# & Emotion Facts

# 7-Day Self-Care Challenge for Kids

- Day 1: Try a new deep breathing exercise.
- Day 2: Draw or journal about your emotions.
- Day 3: Set up a cozy calm-down space.
- Day 4: Do a fun movement activity (yoga, dancing, or stretching).
- Day 5: Practice a positive self-talk mantra.
- Day 6: Listen to calming music and describe how it makes you feel.
- Day 7: Share one thing you're grateful for.

# Fun Facts About Emotions & The Brain

- The amygdala, a small part of the brain, plays a big role in processing emotions like fear and excitement.
- Smiling, even when you don't feel happy, can actually trick your brain into boosting your mood.
- Hugging someone you trust releases oxytocin, a hormone that helps reduce stress.
- Kids who practice mindfulness have better focus and emotional control.
- Naming emotions out loud can help reduce their intensity

# Interactive Games for Emotion Regulation

- **Emotion Charades:** Act out emotions and have others guess what they are.
- **Feelings Match-Up:** Match emotion words to facial expressions or situations.
- **Calm-Down Dice:** Roll a dice and do the calming activity it lands on.
- **Storytelling Challenge:** Make up a short story about a character learning to manage emotions.

# Bonus Tools: Printables and Activities

All bonus worksheets, emotion regulation tools, and parent resources featured in this guide can be downloaded in PDF format for FREE at: All Bonus printables can be purchased in PDF format FREE at https://authentikxpressions.etsy.com using code STORM

🛒 Use code STORM at checkout to receive your free downloads.

Your journey through Parenting the Storm doesn't end here—take the tools with you and keep building calm, connection, and confidence at home.

# Bonus Tools:
# Printables and Activities

1. **Emotion Wheel Worksheet**
2. **Feelings Journal Page**
3. **Calm-Down Cards**
4. **Positive Affirmation Cards**
Encourage kids to read one aloud each morning or when they need a boost.
5. **Emotion Charades Game**
6. **My Safe Space Drawing Sheet**
Let kids design and draw their ideal calm-down corner, complete with items that help them feel safe and cozy.
7. **Calm-Down Dice:** Roll a dice and do the calming activity it lands on.
8. **Emotion Bingo**
As kids recognize and name these emotions in themselves or others throughout the day, they mark them off. A fun way to boost emotional awareness!
9. **Breathing Board Game**
10. **Parent Reflection Page**
Take time to check in with yourself.
Use this page weekly to support your own growth alongside your child's.
11. **Family Emotion Check-In Calendar**
12. **Family Emotions Pledge**
Create a shared family commitment to emotional growth. You can print and sign it together:
13. **Our Family Emotion Pledge**
Keep this pledge visible as a reminder that everyone's emotions are welcome and important.
14. **Emotion Star Certificate**
Celebrate your child's progress with an emotion-themed certificate.
Customize with their name and reason for celebration:
Hang it up to honor their hard work!
15. **Kindness & Feelings Tracker Template**
16. **My Feelings Toolbox Template**
17. **Coloring Pages**

# Feelings Wheel

Color the wheel to reflect the emotion

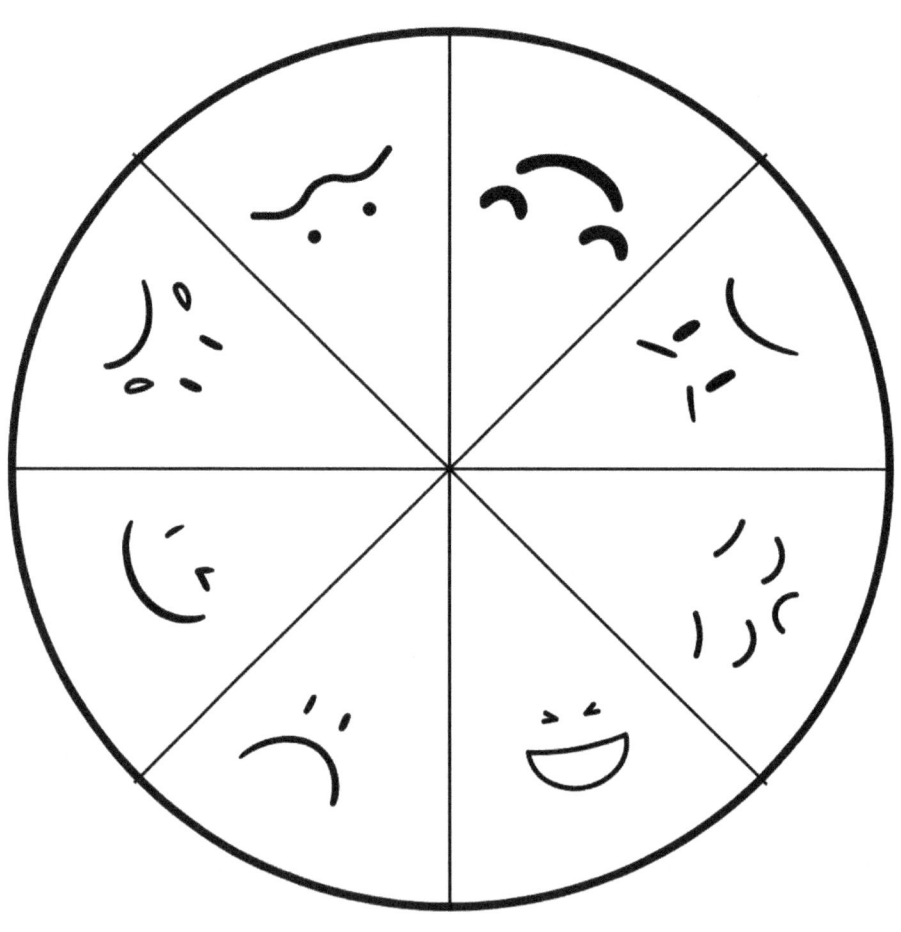

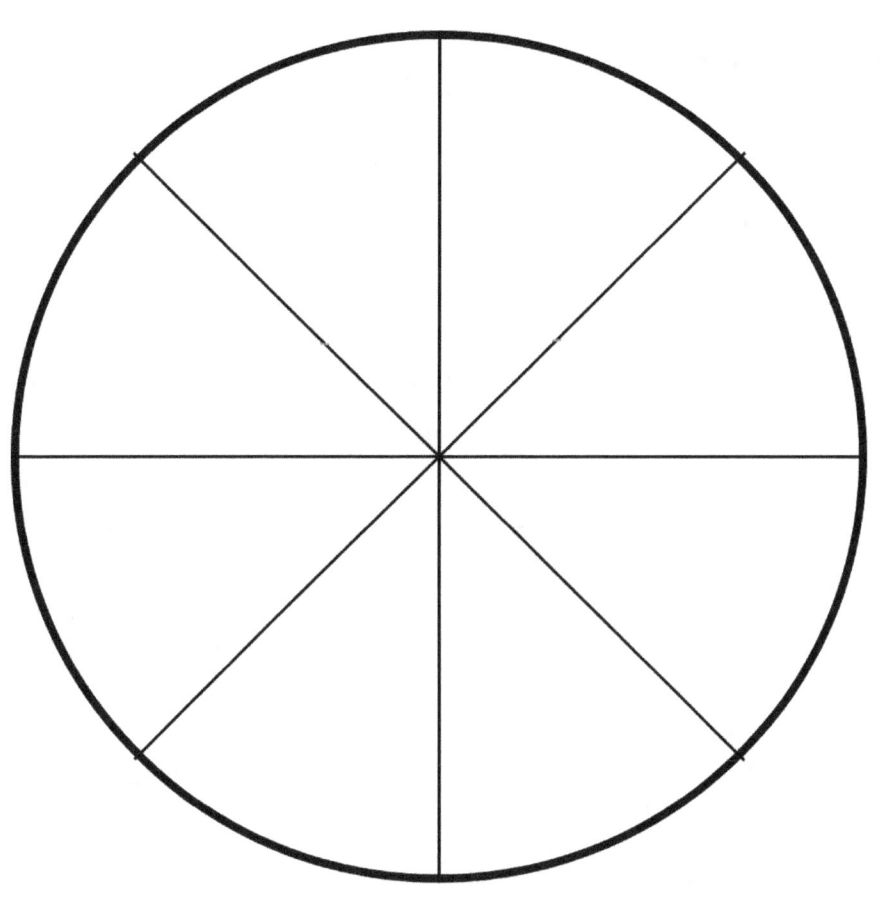

# Identify the Feelings

_____

_____

_____

_____

_____

_____

_____

_____

# JOURNAL

- Today I felt... _____

- Something that made me happy was...
  _____
  _____

- When I was upset, I...
  _____

  _____

  _____

- One thing I'm proud of is...
  _____

# CALMING STRATEGY CARDS

## Balloon Breaths

Blow up a pretend bolloon.

## Magic Coloring

Color away the stress

## Butterfly Hugs

Give yourself a hug!

## Squeeze & Release

## Five Senses Check-In

What do you see, hear, smell, feel, and taste?

## Cozy Corner Time

Take a break in your calm space

## Dance It Out

Move your mood!

## Glitter Jar Watch

Watch the sparkies settie

## Draw Your Feelings

Turn feelings into pictures

## Positive Power Talk
I am strong
Say something kind to yourself

## Stretch & Grow

Stretch like your favorite animal!

## Bubble Breathing

Pretend you're blowing bubbles

# CALMING STRATEGY CARDS

# AFFIRMATION CARDS

I am
brave.

I can
handle
big feelings.

It's okay
to make
mistakes.

I am
learning
every day.

# AFFIRMATION CARDS

# Emotion Charades Game

Write different emotions on slips of paper. Take turns acting them out while others guess. Great for building emotional vocabulary!

| | | |
|---|---|---|
| HAPPY | JOY | DISGUST |
| SAD | MAD | SURPRISED |
| ANGRY | FEAR | ENVY |
| ANXIOUS | IRRITATED | AFRAID |
| CHEERFUL | LOVED | UNSURE |
| EXCITED | ANNOYED | PROUD |
| DEPRESSED | ASHAMED | |

CUT OUT THE WORDS AND USE THEM IN YOUR GAME OR WRITE YOUR OWN WORDS AND CUT THEM OUT.

| | | |
|---|---|---|
| | | |
| | | |
| | | |
| | | |
| | | |
| | | |
| | | |

# My Safe Space
# Drawing Sheet

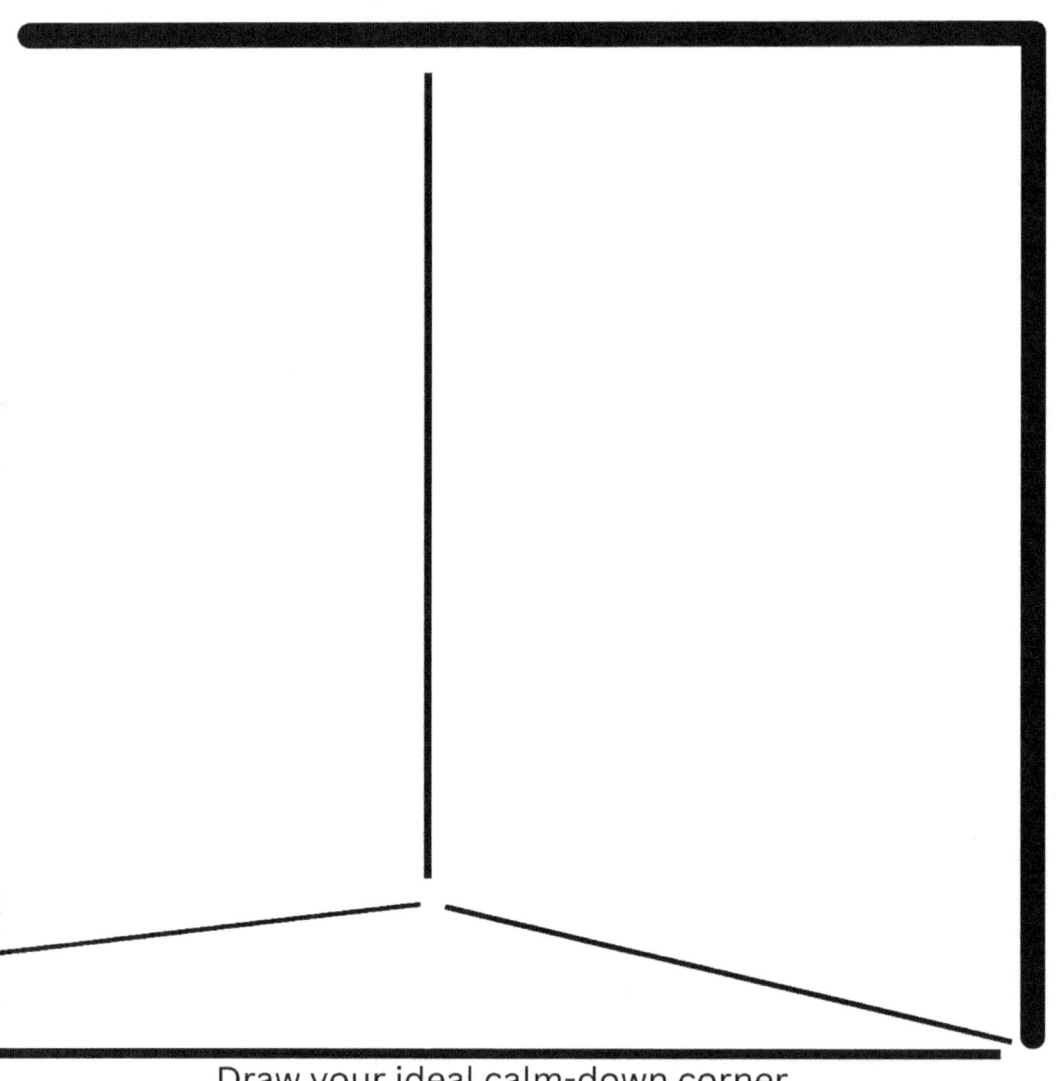

Draw your ideal calm-down corner,
complete with items that help them
feel safe and cozy.

Cut out the dice and fold along the lines . Use tape to connect

Count to 10

Journal how you feel

Square breathing

Tell yourself something positive

Use a calming jar

Dance to your favorite song

**Calm-Down Dice:**
Roll a dice and do the calming activity it lands on.

# Cut out the dice and fold along the lines . Use tape to connect

# EMOTION BINGO

| | | |
|---|---|---|
| happy | sad | angry |
| bored | worried | surprised |
| frustrated | proud | excited |
| shy | nervous | embarrassed |
| scared | hopeful | guilty |

Get 3 diagnal, 5 down or 3 across
to get BINGO

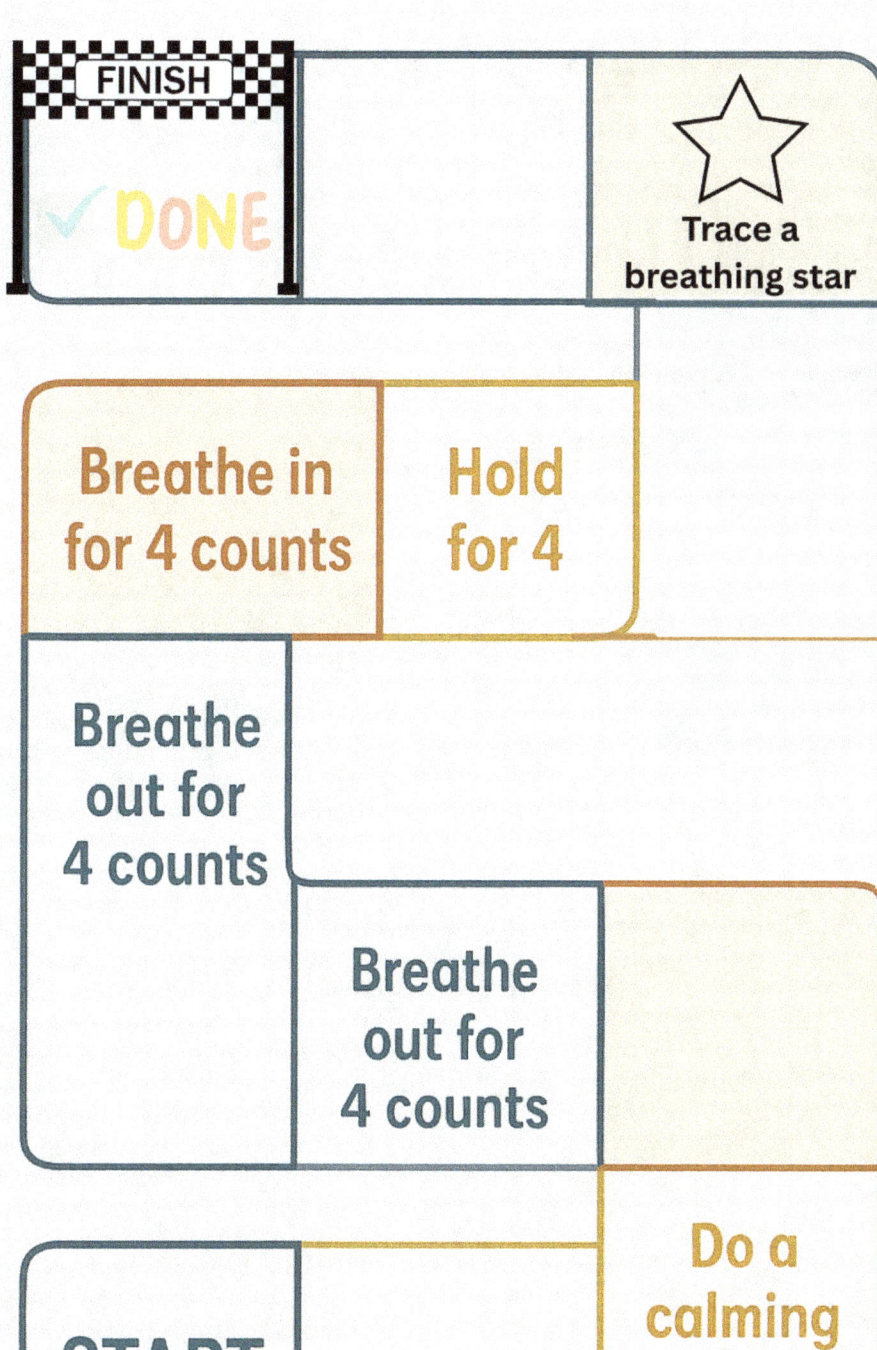

FINISH
✓ DONE

Trace a breathing star

Breathe in for 4 counts

Hold for 4

Breathe out for 4 counts

Breathe out for 4 counts

START

Do a calming stretch

# PARENT JOURNALING

**Take time to check in with yourself.
Prompts include:**

- One way I modeled emotion regulation this week:

- A challenging parenting moment and how I handled it:

- One small thing I can do to care for myself this week:

# Family Emotion Check-In Calendar

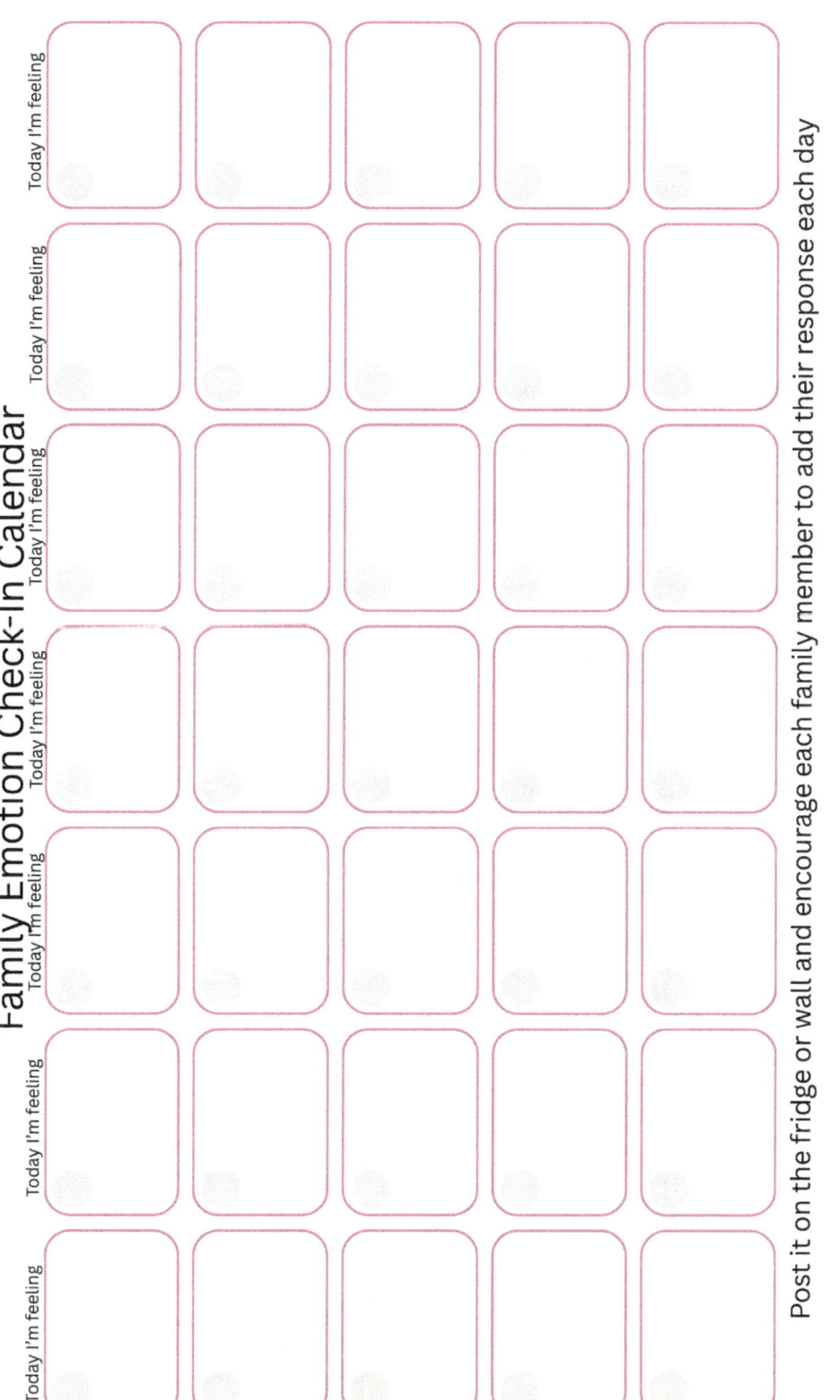

Today I'm feeling

Today I'm feeling

Today I'm feeling

Today I'm feeling

Today I'm feeling

Today I'm feeling

Today I'm feeling

Post it on the fridge or wall and encourage each family member to add their response each day

# Kindness & Feelings Tracker Template

Helped someone else

Talked about a feeling

Used a calming tool

Made someone smile

Used Kind words

Post it on the fridge or wall and at the end of the week, reflect together on what they're proud of.

# My Feelings Toolbox

What helps me when I'm mad:

What helps me when I'm sad:

What helps me when I'm nervous:

What helps me when I'm _____

Decorate or draw your actual "toolbox

# OUR FAMILY
# EMOTION PLEDGE

We will respect all feelings—big and small.
We will use our words to express how we feel.
We will listen to each other with kindness.
We will take deep breaths and use calm-down tools.
We will support each other when emotions feel hard.

SIGNED

SIGNED

# EMOTION STAR CERTIFICATE

THIS CERTIFICATE IS AWARDED TO

for showing amazing growth in handling big feelings with courage and care.

THERAPIST

PARENT

# Appendix

# RESOURCES

Additional things you can do to assist you in your time of anxiety is to have reminders that you can rely on when thought blocking occurs. Reminders could be bracelets, anxiety candles, essential oils, create an anxiety plan and maybe learning some mindfulness activities that work for you. Mindfulness activities are deep breathing (Square/box breathing, progressive relaxation, belly breathing, simple breathing), yoga, meditation (Guided), or structure your day with positive task.

All appendix worksheets, emotion regulation tools, and parent resources featured in this guide can be downloaded in PDF format at:
All appendix printables can be purchased in PDF format at
https://authentikxpressions.etsy.com

This site allows you to seek out counselors in your area that would be helpful to you, for you and you can view their profile before booking an appointment.

**Psychologytoday.com**

# Psychology Today

## Your insurance carrier

Most insurances can refer you to a counselor to assist you with your needs. Call the number on the back of your insurance card and inquire about counseling services.

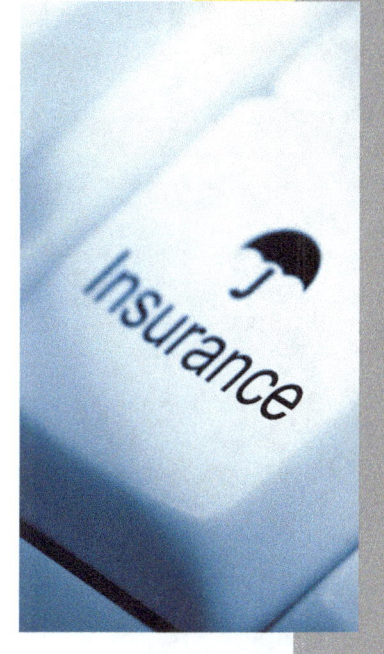

# Your Doctor's office

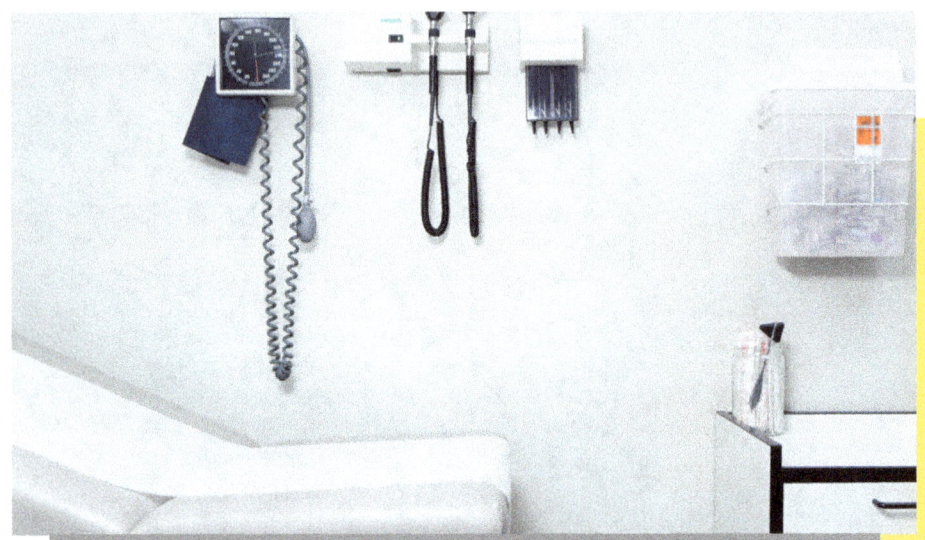

### Your doctor's office

Most doctor's offices have referrals to counselors in the area you may be able to reach out to for services. Contact them today and inquire about referrals to counselors in your area.

# 988 | SUICIDE & CRISIS LIFELINE

## 24/7 CALL, TEXT, CHAT

1-800-273-8255

This lifeline will not only assist you with brief counseling services to help you in the moment but they can also provide referral information for counselors in your area.

# Ask a Friend

**Reach out for Support**
This option requires you to talk to someone about how you are feeling and will lead you to referrals and support you are seeking.

# TOOLS

# Active Grounding

---

- Grounding yourself is really like placing yourself in the here and now. We typically operate in the past or the future. A lot of our thoughts and actions are rooted from past things things that have happened in the past or things that we believe will happen in the future.

- Active Grounding brings you into the present moment where you're able to realize that you are ok in that moment. Your focus shifts to what is around you currently.

# GROUNDING

Active Grounding techniques can be done in any place. Active grounding is the act of you physically doing something to bring yourself more present. Many grounding techniques are mindfulness techniques but the active grounding allows you to focus your attention on an activity rather than trying to be mindful in a moment of fear and chaos.

# 3 & 1

This grounding technique requires you to choose 3 colors and 1 shape. You then take the chosen color (ex: RED) and you name everything that is red in the room or around you.

*The key is to name those things OUT LOUD. Verbally say those things you see.*

When there is nothing else red now name everything that is (ex: GREEN) name those things OUT LOUD. When there is nothing else green
Now name everything that is (ex: BLUE) name those things OUT LOUD. When there is nothing else blue
Now name everything that is in the shape of a (ex: rectangle) name every rectangle you see OUT LOUD.

# 3 & 1

## Active Grounding

It is very important that you verbalizes things out loud. This is the active part of grounding.
As you are naming things your anxiety level is decreasing and you are now able to think better because thought blocking is no longer an issue.

Your mind is clear of the things that was causing anxiety and you are now present and in the room with those things that are those colors and those shapes.

42

# 5 Senses Grounding

For this grounding technique, you will focus on your 5 senses. Most of us have 5 senses we rely on daily. This technique forces you to focus on those senses to bring you into the here and now. Look around the room or place you are in and verbally call out things that are connected to your 5 senses.

First you call out 5 things you can see with your eyes (sense #1).

Next call out 4 things you can feel (sense #2).

Now call out 3 things you can hear (sense #3).

Now call out 2 things you can smell (sense #4).

Lastly call out 1 thing you can taste (sense #5).

5-4-3-2-1

Many times if you are experiencing anxiety you have been crying and some of your senses are difficult to use such as your sense of smell and taste.

In those instances you would name things that you wish you could smell or taste.

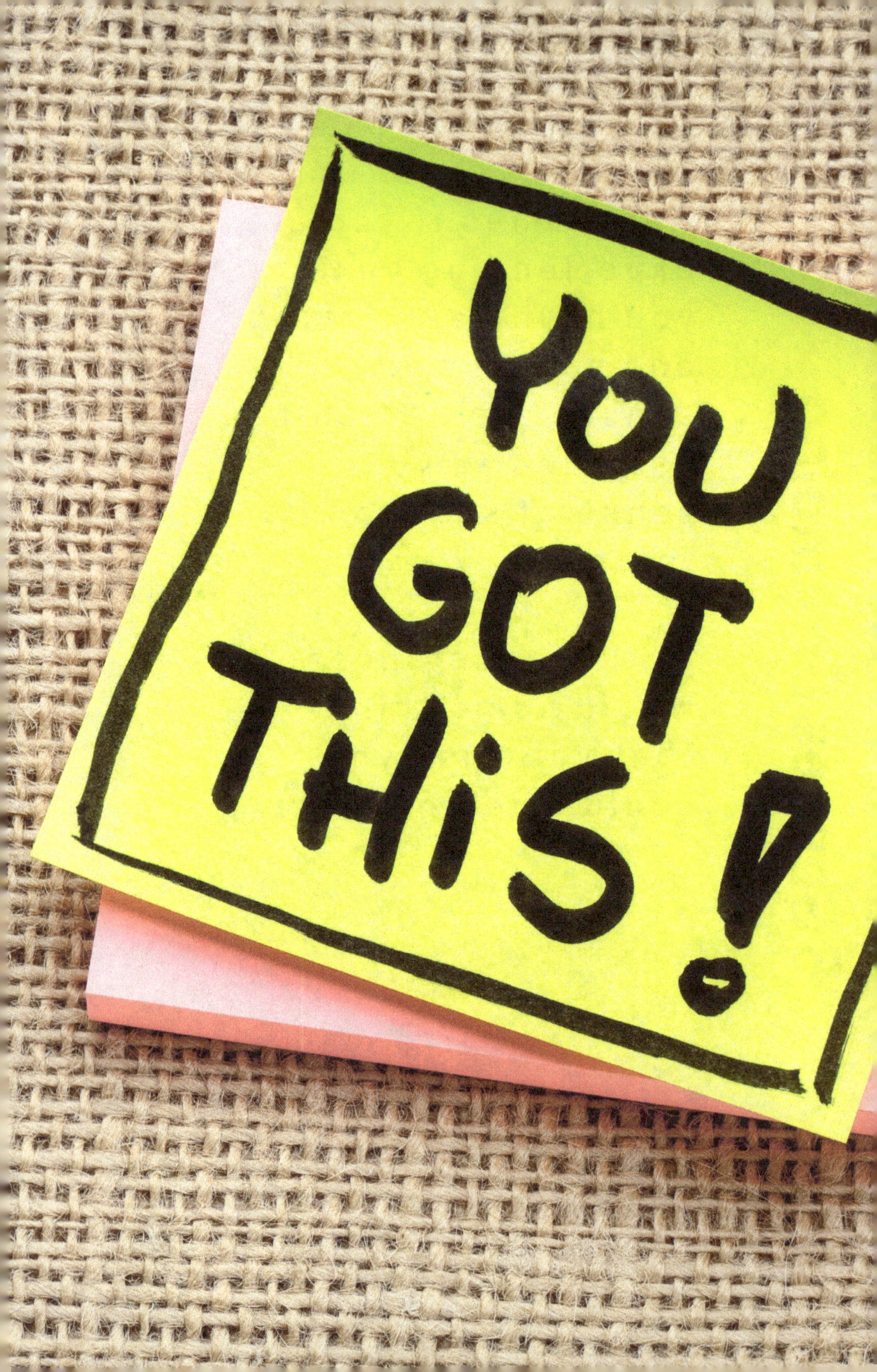
YOU
GOT
THIS!

# Anxiety Tool kit available at:

https://authentikxpressions.etsy.com

---

Anxiety tool kit contains:
Anxiety cards with
-5-4-3-2-1 grounding
-3 & 1 grounding
-Reminder cards of what to do to decrease anxiety
-Coping skills cards
-Selfcare cards
-Mindfulness cards
-An anxiety candle
-An essential oil
- Essential oil inhaler
-54321 reminder bracelet
-Chakra/Lava stone bracelet
-(2) Breathing whistle w/ case & cleaning brush
-(4) Reusable ice cubes
-Affirmation cards

---

# Thank you for your PURCHASE

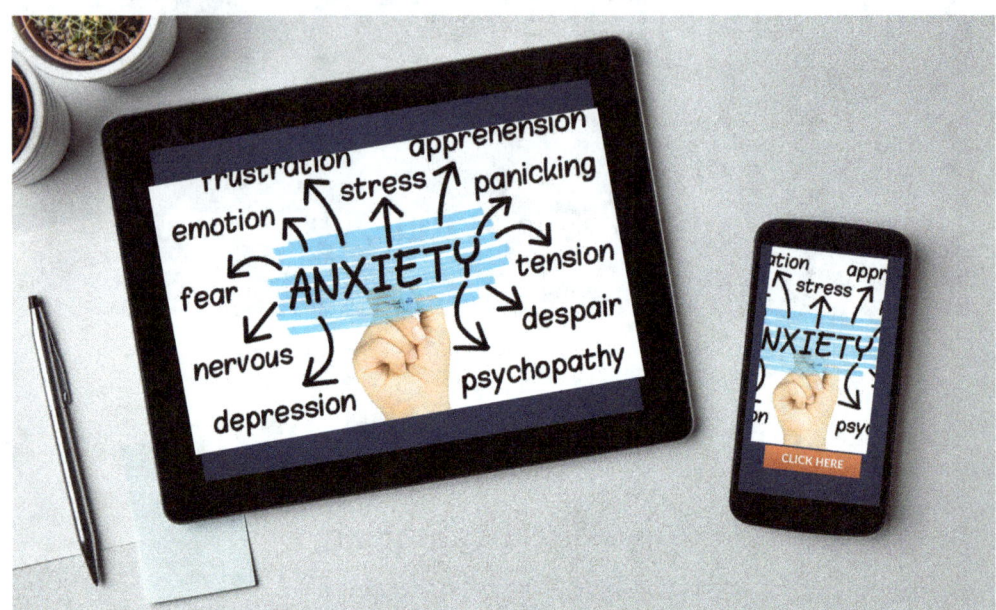

Tell us what you thought of the book on our Facebook or instagram page.

  /maddtherapy

# Active Grounding Countdown Method

| | | | | |
|---|---|---|---|---|
| NAME **5** | NAME **4** | NAME **3** | NAME **2** | NAME **1** |
| things you | things you | things you | things you | thing you |
|  |  |  |  |  |
| See | feel | hear | smell | taste |

# Active Grounding
# Colors & Shapes Method

**Step #1:**  Pick 1 color

**Step #2:**  Name everything in the room that is that color

**Step #3:**  Pick a 2nd color

**Step #4:**  Name everything in the room that is that color

**Step #5:**  Pick a 3rd color

**Step #6:**  Name everything in the room that is that color

**Step #7:**  Pick 1 shape

**Step #8:**  Name everything in the room that is that shape

Now try a coping skill...

# Triangle
# Breathing

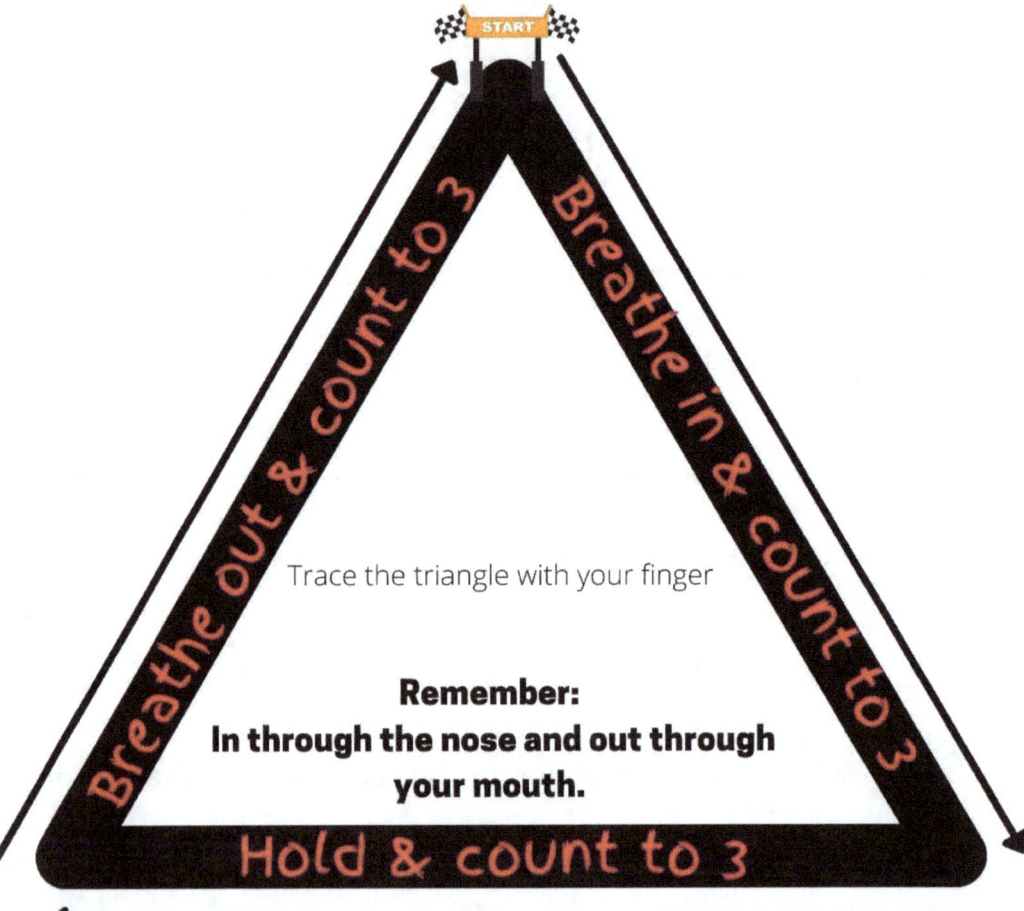

Breathe in & count to 3

Breathe out & count to 3

Trace the triangle with your finger

**Remember:**
**In through the nose and out through**
**your mouth.**

Hold & count to 3

As you breathe in you breathe in stating I am feeling calm you breathe out stating I am releasing my anxiety you breathe in new energy you breathe out releasing worries

# Square
# Breathing

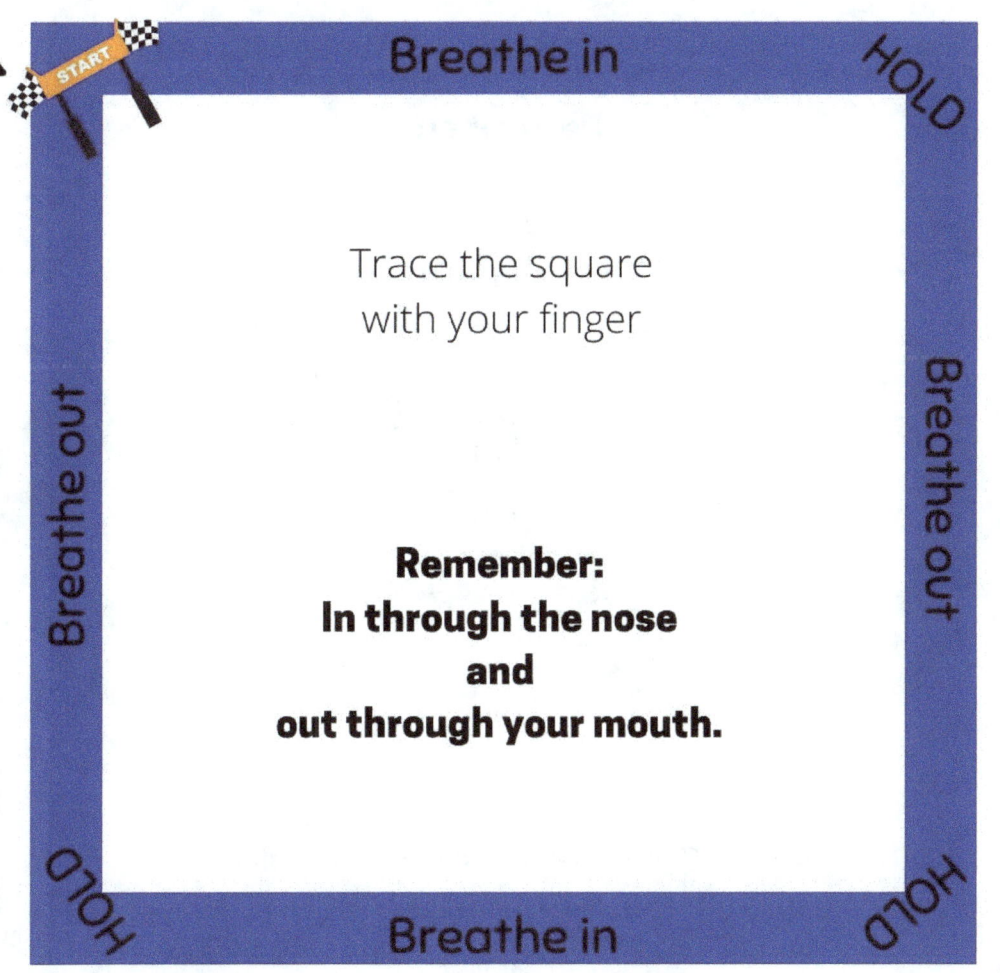

**START**

Breathe in

HOLD

Breathe out

Trace the square
with your finger

Breathe out

**Remember:
In through the nose
and
out through your mouth.**

HOLD

Breathe in

HOLD

As you breathe in you breathe in stating I am feeling calm
you breathe out stating I am releasing my anxiety you
breathe in new energy you breathe out releasing worries

# Infinity Breathing

Trace the infinity with your finger

**Remember:
In through the nose
and
out through your mouth.**

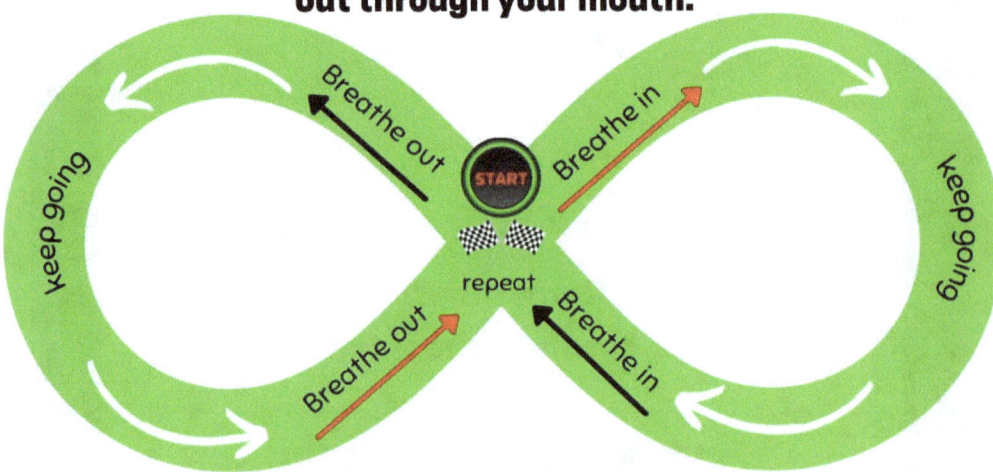

As you breathe in you breathe in stating I am
feeling calm you breathe out stating I am
releasing my anxiety you breathe in new energy
you breathe out releasing worries

# Bonus

# Living in Fear of Excellence

Podcast Live - Ep. Living in Fear of Excellence

with Wesley Morgan, LPC & Keisha McDonald

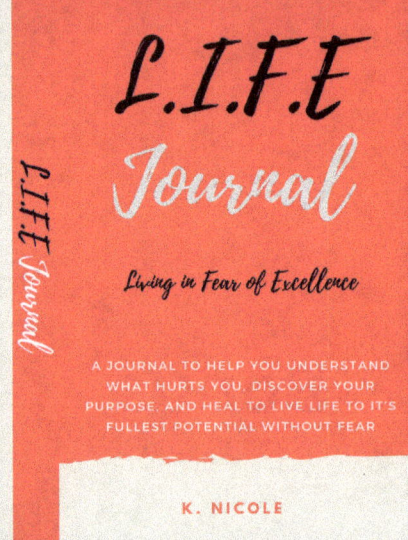

07.50                                                    10.00

## STREAMING NOW

### EVERYTHING RENEWED

# SCAN THE CODE
# TO LISTEN

# ANXIETY RELEASE

**Author:** Keisha McDonald
**Page count:** 86 pages
**Publisher:** AmourLegaci Publishing
**Language:** English
**Format:** Paperback and
**Available on:** Amazon, Barnes&Noble, AmourLegaci.com, Ingram spark and other major book retailers
**Bulk orders on Ingram spark and Amazon**

Release Anxiety is your personal guide to letting go of fear, worry, and emotional tension. Packed with practical exercises, calming techniques, and mindset shifts, this book empowers you to take control of your anxiety rather than letting it control you. Whether you're dealing with daily stress or deep-rooted overwhelm, Release Anxiety offers the tools and encouragement you need to breathe deeper, think clearer, and live with greater peace and confidence.

## Highlights:

- Emotion Regulation
- Body Map
- Feelings & Emotions
- Selfcare

**Paperback:**
978-1735612510

**Ebook:**
978-1735612515

**Keisha McDonald, MS, MA, LPC**
**AUTHOR, ENTREPRENUER, THERAPIST, TRAINER**
AMOURLEGACIPUBLISHING.COM

@ AMOURLEGACIPUBLISHING@GMAIL.COM

f FACEBOOK.COM/AMOURLEGACI

☎ 6163172710

# THE EMOTION COMPASS

## BONUS:

**Worksheets available on Etsy shop**
https://authentikxpressions.etsy.com

This guide offers practical tools, empowering techniques Unlocking Self-Awareness for Emotional Wellness. This workbook will help you find practical tools and exercises designed to help you process and manage your emotions effectively. Whether you're exploring joy, navigating sadness, embracing peace, or confronting anxiety, each page offers guidance to cultivate emotional intelligence and foster personal growth.

THE
EMOTION
COMPASS

Navigating Your Feelings to Find Balance

KEISHA MCDONALD, LPC

## Paperback:
978-1-955234-10-8

Author: Keisha McDonald
Page count: 102 pages
Publisher: AmourLegaci Publishing
Language: English
Format: Paperback
Available on: **Amazon, Barnes&Noble, AmourLegacipublishing.com**
**Bulk orders on Barnes & Noble and Amazon**

**Keisha McDonald, MS, MA, LPC**
**AUTHOR, ENTREPRENUER, THERAPIST, TRAINER**
**AMOURLEGACIPUBLISHING.COM**

 **AMOURLEGACIPUBLISHING@GMAIL.COM**

 **FACEBOOK.COM/AMOURLEGACI**

 **6163172710**

# About the Author

Therapy is a process of growth and self-discovery, and can be experienced in various forms. I promote behavioral transformation by encouraging a positive outlook and the adoption of new attitudes and relationships.

I am a therapist who strives to empower others to obtain successful outcomes as they are faced with life challenges. I work with individuals experiencing anxiety, depression, self esteem, foster care related issues and child and adolescent trauma.

I operate a practice called MADD Therapy in Michigan. I also work with clients through Renewed Counseling in Michigan. I have extensive knowledge & experience working with clients and families who are struggling with anxiety, depression, adjustment disorders, foster care related issues and child trauma. I also have additional training in child and adolescent trauma, cognitive behavioral therapy, dialectical behavioral therapy and trauma focused cognitive behavioral therapy.

I use expressive arts in addition to elements of cognitive behavioral, motivational interviewing, solution focused, mindfulness and other therapies to help clients.

 maddtherapy